New IT Technology Issues Facing CIOs

How CIOs Can Stay On Top Of The Changes In The Technology That Powers The Company

"Practical, proven techniques that will show you how to use technology to make your company more successful"

Dr. Jim Anderson

Published by:
Blue Elephant Consulting
Tampa, Florida

Copyright © 2016 by Dr. Jim Anderson

All rights reserved. No part of this book may be reproduced of transmitted in any form or by any means, electronic or mechanical, including photocopying, recording or by any information storage and retrieval system without written permission of the publisher, except for inclusion of brief quotations in a review.

Printed in the United States of America

Library of Congress Control Number: 2016920720

ISBN-13: 978-1541096240
ISBN-10: 154109624X

Warning – Disclaimer

The purpose of this book is to educate and entertain. This book does not promise or guarantee that anyone following the ideas, tips, suggestions, techniques or strategies will be successful. The author, publisher and distributor(s) shall have neither liability nor responsibility to anyone with respect to any loss or damage caused, or alleged to be caused, directly or indirectly by the information contained in this book.

Recent Books By The Author

Product Management

- Managing Your Product Manager Career: How Product Managers Can Find And Succeed In The Right Job

- How Product Managers Can Sell More Of Their Product: Tips & Techniques For Product Managers To Better Understand How To Sell Their Product

- Product Development Lessons For Product Managers: How Product Managers Can Create Successful Products

Public Speaking

- How To Organize A Speech In Order To Make Your Point: How to put together a speech that will capture and hold your audience's attention

- Changing How You Speak To Overcome Your Fear Of Speaking: Change techniques that will transform a speech into a memorable event

CIO Skills

- Keeping The Barbarians Out: How CIOs Can Secure Their Department and Company: Tips And Techniques For

CIOs To Use In Order To Secure Both Their IT Department And Their Company

- What CIOs Need To Know In Order To Successfully Manage An IT Department: Decision Making Skills That Every CIO Needs To Have In Order To Be Able To Make The Right Choices

- How CIOs Can Make Innovation Happen: Tips And Techniques For CIOs To Use In Order To Make Innovation Happen In Their IT Department

IT Manager Skills

- How To Build High Performance IT Teams: Tips And Techniques That IT Managers Can Use In Order To Develop Productive Teams

- Building The Perfect Team: What Staffing Skills Do IT Managers Need?: Tips And Techniques That IT Managers Can Use In Order To Correctly Staff Their Teams

- Secrets Of Effective Leadership For IT Managers: Tips And Techniques That IT Managers Can Use In Order To Develop Leadership Skills

Negotiating

- Exploring How To Get The Deal That You Want In A Negotiation: How To Develop The Skill Of Exploring

What Is Possible In A Negotiation In Order To Reach The Best Possible Deal

- Use The Power Of Arguing To Win Your Next Negotiation: How To Develop The Skill Of Effective Arguing In A Negotiation In Order To Get The Best Possible Outcome

Miscellaneous

- How To Heal A Broken Leg – Fast!: Understanding how to deal with a broken leg in order to start walking again quickly

- How Software Defined Networking (SDN) Is Going To Change Your World Forever: The Revolution In Network Design And How It Affects

Note: See a complete list of books by Dr. Jim Anderson at the back of this book.

Acknowledgements

Any book like this one is the result of years of real-world work experience. In my over 25 years of working for 7 different firms, I have met countless fantastic people and I've been mentored by some truly exceptional ones. Although I've probably forgotten some of the people who made me the person that I am today, here is my attempt to finally give them the recognition that they so truly deserve:

- Thomas P. Anderson
- Art Puett
- Bobbi Marshall
- Bob Boggs

Dr. Jim Anderson

This book is dedicated to my family: Lori, Maddie, Nick, and Ben. None of this would have been possible without their constant love and support.

Thanks for always believing in me and providing me with the strength to always be willing to go out there and be my best for you.

Speaking.   Negotiating.   Managing.   Marketing.

Table Of Contents

CIOS HAVE TO MASTER THE WORLD OF CHANGING TECHNOLOGY 9

ABOUT THE AUTHOR 11

CHAPTER 1: GARTNER REVEALS TOP 10 TECHNOLOGIES 16

CHAPTER 2: PAINT BY NUMBERS — THE CIO'S NEW JOB.................19

CHAPTER 3: CRM NEWS: THE BUSINESS OF INFORMATION TECHNOLOGY IS CHANGING 22

CHAPTER 4: LONDON STOCK EXCHANGE GLITCH – COULD CLOUD COMPUTING HAVE SAVED THE DAY?..25

CHAPTER 5: HEALTH CARE CHANGES: IS IT ENOUGH? 28

CHAPTER 6: THE PROBLEM WITH APPLE: PRODUCT OR PLATFORM?31

CHAPTER 7: PRACTICAL IT CLOUDS: WHAT TO DO AFTER THE HYPE.34

CHAPTER 8: UNIFIED COMMUNICATIONS IS AN OPPORTUNITY FOR CIOS TO SHOW THEIR VALUE 37

CHAPTER 9: FIRST-MOVER ADVANTAGE: COMPLEX-EVENT PROCESSING IS WHAT CIOS NEED...41

CHAPTER 10: WEB 3.0 IS COMING – ARE CIOS READY? 45

CHAPTER 11: CIO CLOUD COMPUTING 101: WHO ARE THE PLAYERS? 49

CHAPTER 12: CIO CLOUD COMPUTING 101: WHY USE THE CLOUD? .53

CIOs Have To Master The World Of Changing Technology

It's always been known that the job of being CIO is a tough job. One of the reasons that this job is so hard to do well is because we stand on shifting ground. The technology that we use goes out of style and then gets replaced by new technology almost overnight.

One of your tasks as CIO is to be able to take a look at new and emerging technologies and determine which of these will impact your company. Due to the size of this task, it is often helpful to go to outside sources to get help in evaluating all of the new technologies. Almost all of the emerging technologies involve massive amounts of data. How to store, process, and create results from this data is one critical new technology that all CIOs will have to master.

In the world of IT, big projects make up a lot of what we do. Things like implementing new and novel customer relationship management (CRM) systems or special purpose applications like have been done for the London Stock Exchange are what we do. However, once done, we are then responsible for ensuring that our creations stay up and running.

Decisions are a key part of being a CIO. No matter if it's trying to decide between an Apple based product or a Windows product, these are never easy decisions. As changes have rolled through the world of healthcare, CIOs have been drawn in and have had to make many different decisions about how systems should operate.

Keeping your company out in front of the competition is part of the job of being CIO. What this entails these days is that you need to be able to implement complex-event processing and start to move key business applications to the cloud.

For more information on what it takes to be a great CIO, check out my blog, The Accidental Successful CIO, at:

www.TheAccidentalSuccessfulCIO.com

Good luck!

- Dr. Jim Anderson

About The Author

I must confess that I never set out to be a CIO. When I went to school, I studied Computer Science and thought that I'd get a nice job programming and that would be that. Well, at least part of that plan worked out!

My first job was working for Boeing on their F/A-18 fighter jet program. I spent my days programming fighter jet software in assembly language and I loved it. The U.S. government decided to save some money and went looking for other countries to sell this plane to. This put me into an unfamiliar role: I started to meet with foreign military officials and I ended up having to manage groups of engineers who were working on international projects.

Time moved on and so did I. I found myself working for Siemens, the big German telecommunications company. They were making phone switches and selling them to the seven U.S. phone companies. The problem was that the switches were too complicated. Customers couldn't tell the difference between one complicated phone switch from another complicated phone switch. Once again I found myself working with the sales and marketing teams to find ways to make the great technology that the engineers had developed understandable to both internal and external customers.

I've spent over 25 years working as an senior IT professional for both big companies and startups. This has given me an opportunity to learn what it takes to manage and IT department in ways that allow it to maximize its output while becoming a valuable part of the overall company.

I now live in Tampa Florida where I spend my time managing my consulting business, Blue Elephant Consulting, teaching college courses at the University of South Florida, and traveling to work with companies like yours to share the knowledge that I have about how to create and manage successful IT departments.

I'm always available to answer questions and I can be reached at:

Dr. Jim Anderson
Blue Elephant Consulting
Email: jim@BlueElephantConsulting.com
Facebook: http://goo.gl/1TVoK
Web: **www.BlueElephantConsulting.com**

"**Unforgettable communication skills that will set your ideas free...**"

Create IT Departments That Are Productive And A Valuable Asset To The Rest Of The Company!

Dr. Jim Anderson is available to provide training and coaching on the topics that are the most important to people who have to manage IT departments: how can I build a productive IT department (and keep it together) while at the same time providing the rest of the company with the IT services that they need?

Dr. Anderson believes that in order to both learn and remember what he says, speakers need to laugh. Each one of his speeches is full of fun and humor so that what he says "sticks" with everyone.

Dr. Anderson's CIO SkillsTraining Includes:

1. How to identify and attract the right type of IT workers to your IT department.
2. How to build relationships with the company's senior management in order to get the support that you need?
3. How to stay on top of changing technology and security issues so that you never get surprised?

Dr. Jim Anderson works with over 100 customers per year. To invite Dr. Anderson to work with you, contact him at:

Phone: 813-418-6970 or
Email: jim@BlueElephantConsulting.com

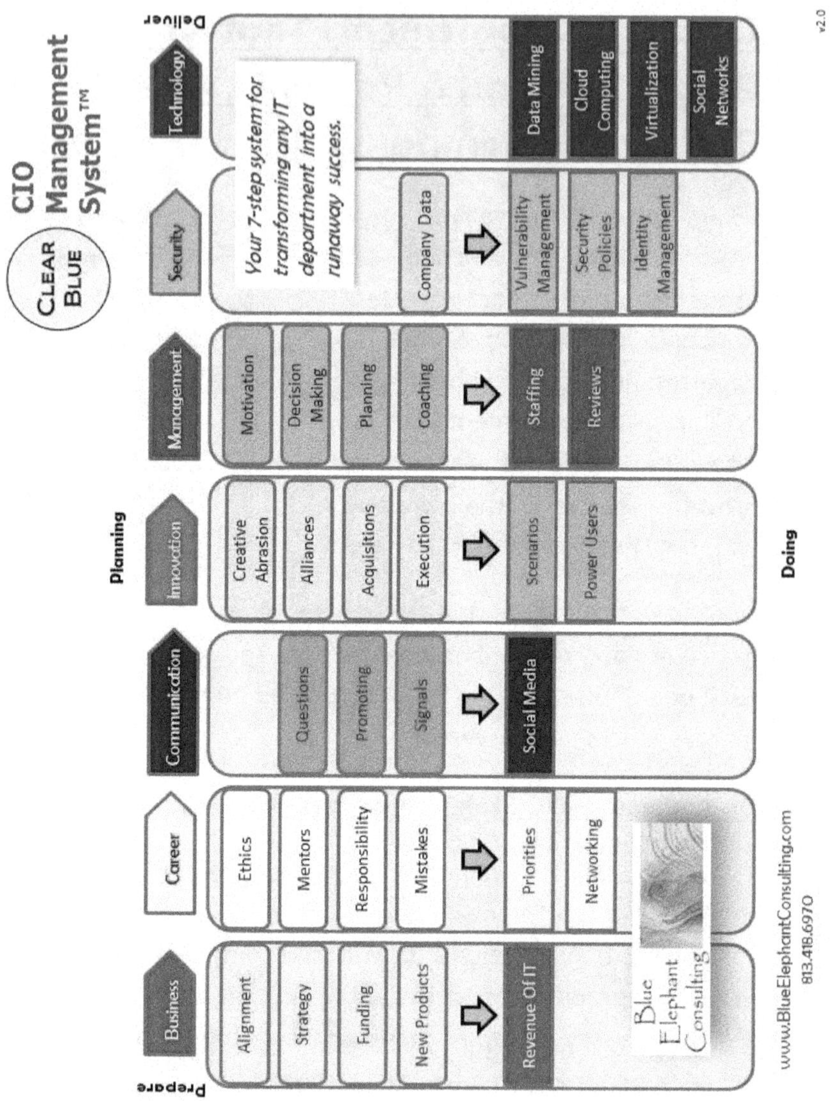

The **Clear Blue CIO Management System™** has been created to provide CIOs and senior IT managers with a clear roadmap for how to manage an IT department. This system shows CIOs what needs to be done and in what order to do it.

Chapter 1

Gartner Reveals Top 10 Technologies

Chapter 1: Gartner Reveals Top 10 Technologies

The good folks over at the Gartner Group have revealed the top 10 technologies that they believe will change the world over the next four years:

1. Multicore and hybrid processors
2. Virtualization and fabric computing
3. Social networks and social software
4. Cloud computing and cloud/Web platforms
5. Web mashups
6. User Interface
7. Ubiquitous computing
8. Contextual computing
9. Augmented reality
10. Semantics

What caught my attention were items 1-4. I think that Gartner got it right this time around. Muticore servers and virtualization will mean that firms will need fewer boxes and apps can be easily moved from box to box (and right out the door to an outsourced data center).

Workplace social networks and cloud computing means that the need for a centralized IT department will go away. Firms will no longer need to own/maintain the boxes that they use to run their firm's apps. With no need to touch a box, there will be no need to have the IT staff co-located with the boxes. Oh, oh — can you hear your job going away?

What does this all mean, and more importantly what should a successful IT staffer (or CIO) do today? The key to your future success is to understand how IT is going to change and what you need to do to change with it. IT is going to become much more about information and how it can be used to help the business

Chapter 2

Paint By Numbers — The CIO's New Job

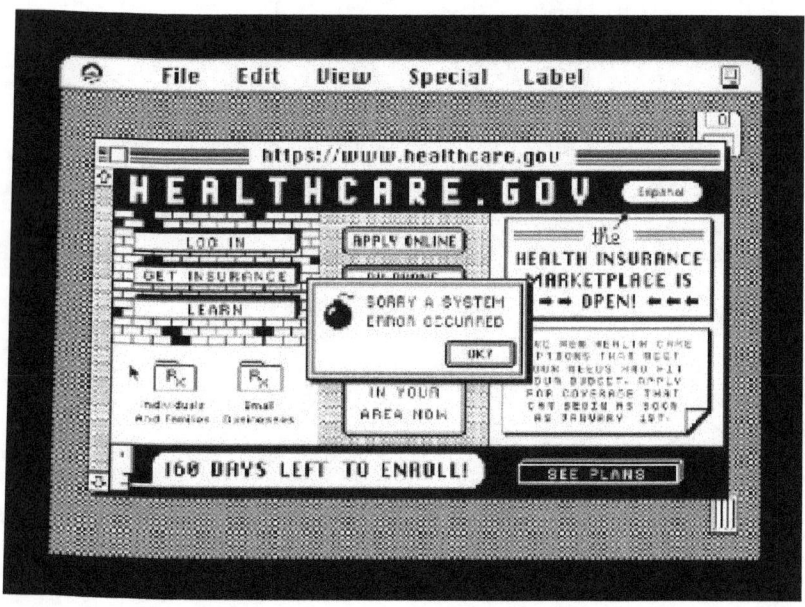

grow and prosper. This IT function is going to leave the IT department as we know it today and will migrate into the business unit itself. What this means to you is that you need to know what your firm does, and even more importantly, how it does it. The next question will be what information is needed by the business units to improve how they do their work. This is what tomorrow's IT staff will provide. Thanks Gartner for the peek into the future!

Chapter 2: Paint By Numbers — The CIO's New Job

It's becoming more and more clear that the tradition CIO job of spending time on operational issues is quickly becoming out of date. What's a CIO really supposed to be doing with his/her time? The answer, as it's always been, is finding ways for the IT staff to make the business able to do its job better. One relatively new way for a CIO to do this is in the area of quantitative analysis.

Quantitative analysis is the process by which often huge quantities of numbers related to the business, the economy, customers, inventory, etc. are "crunched" through custom algorithms, statistical packages, and home grown code in order to transform information into real world business knowledge that can be used to make educated business decisions.

This type of processing is not easy to do — you have to be very sure that the answers that you are getting are real answers and not just good looking garbage numbers tumbling out of a fancy analysis tool. The ability to make sure the correct processing is being done is the responsibility of the quantitative analytical specialists (the really big brains).

So what role does a CIO play in all of this? Well the quantitative analytical specialists need to live somewhere in the company and since they live and breath the data that only IT can collect for them, often they become part of the IT organization and report to the CIO. The CIO is then responsible for making sure that the correct parts of the company's operations are being monitored and metered so that the analytical specialists get the data that they need.

Getting date can often be the easy part, getting good "clean" data can often be quite difficult to do. Additionally, the CIO will then be responsible for taking the analytical specialists' outputs (which can be quite technical) and presenting them to the rest of the business in a way that they can understand and take action on. The CIO will then become part of the feedback loop as the business asks follow-on questions that can only be answered by additional analysis.

I believe that this type of function is much closer to where CIOs will be as we move forward. The CIO will truly start to deserve the "I" in their title — but it will be their ability to transform information into actionable knowledge that will make them and their department a critical part of the firm's success.

Chapter 3

CRM News: The Business Of Information Technology Is Changing

Chapter 3: CRM News: The Business Of Information Technology Is Changing

With all of the changes that are once again starting to happen in IT, can you imagine how the big boys at SAP/Oracle/etc. (the traditional CRM vendors) are starting to feel? There is starting to be more and more talk about cloud computing and folks are even starting to play around with it — a clear sign of a potential disruptive influence if ever there was one. The arrival of this type of web-based computing threatens to change their business model. We can learn a lot from taking a moment to study their situation.

We've talked about the fact that most firms don't seem to get the biggest bang for the buck from their expensive implementations of CRM systems. As time marches on the IT department is going to get hit with another change when folks start thinking about moving these big applications out to the cloud.

In a recent interview with the Wall Street Journal, Henning Kagermann (CEO of SAP) said that he doesn't see IT departments making this kind of move anytime soon because they are too conservative. The difference between "traditional" CRM and "web-based" CRM is that the web-based solution is designed to make it easier for the sales folks, purchasing folks, etc.

Henning points out that traditional CRM solutions are really designed to be used by the management team — not the front line workers. These workers value system security and reliability over everything else and so he anticipates no significant changes soon.

Henning is a bright guy and I'd tend to agree with his view of the world if it were not for three things:

1. **Options**: New firms will no longer HAVE to deploy CRM applications on their own servers — they can use a cloud. If any of these firms turns into the next Google, then there will be a mad rush to be more like them and that could cause a quick change.

2. **Pricing**: if because of competition between Amazon, Google, and IBM it suddenly becomes so cheap to deploy an application in "the cloud" everything could move out almost overnight.

3. **CIO Innovations**: ultimately a CRM system is only as good as the data that is entered into it. If CIOs take the lead and assume ownership of the quality (and quantity) of data that is entered into the CRM system, then suddenly the value of the system goes through the roof. In order to make this happen, CIOs will need to make the application easy to get to and easy to use — both characteristics are features of web-based applications.

Nothing ever seems to happen overnight; however, a great deal can happen in just a single business quarter. Henning is betting that IT won't see any of these three events happen before SAP has time to create a web version of their product. Let's see how things go...

Chapter 4

London Stock Exchange Glitch – Could Cloud Computing Have Saved The Day?

Chapter 4: London Stock Exchange Glitch – Could Cloud Computing Have Saved The Day?

Just when you think that you have the worst job in IT, a story like this comes along! Last Monday the London Stock Exchange (LSE) experienced a full day outage. Traders who were ready to trade were unable to connect to one of the LSE's main trading applications. No connect, no trading.

If you'll think back about a week or so, you'll realize that Monday was a very important day in stock trading land. The U.S. Government had just stepped in to shore up Fannie Mae and Freddie Mac. What this meant is that over in London, there were lots of traders who wanted to buy/sell British bank stocks because of what they thought the impact of this move would have on British stocks. However, for a full day nobody could trade anything!

The LSE uses a trading program called TradElect which is a 15 month old proprietary application that they've build using Microsoft technology. It appears that the traders were unable to connect to this application and that is why everyone experienced the outage.

The big question is why? Their trading volume grew too quickly and caused their software/hardware capabilities to be exceeded. Although the LSE is not talking, we can probably take some educated guesses at to what went wrong here.

Since TradElect has been in service for 15 months, it's probably not the fault of the functionality of the application. Additionally, since the problem lasted the entire day, clearly the IT team was unable to revert to a previous version of the application in order to fix the problem – so no "upgrade gone wrong" problem here.

My guess is that this is an old fashion "too much volume" problem.

I almost hate to use the term, but could "cloud computing" be the solution for the LSE? Specifically, should they design their apps to run on their servers in their data center but build in an option to expand to additional servers located in some secure cloud in the event that there is a surge in trading like (tried to) happened on Monday? You can never guess at exactly how much computing capacity that you'll need and perhaps this is where the brave new world of cloud computing can shine. Maybe this is a question that the next LSE CIO will have an opportunity to answer...

Chapter 5

Health Care Changes: Is IT Enough?

Chapter 5: Health Care Changes: Is IT Enough?

So here's the $19B question for you: if you were the CIO in charge of the Obama administration's big **health care initiative**, do you think that the "secret sauce" that will make it all work out will be better / more IT?

Just in case you've not been following this developing story, one of the Obama administration's key election promises was to fix the broken U.S. health care system – it costs too much and delivers too little care. A main tenet of how they are proposing to do this is through **IT investments**. The poster child of this massive IT investment is something called Electronic Health Records (EHRs).

The administration is forecasting that using EHRs could save the government **up to $77B annually**! We in IT just LOVE any problem that can be solved by throwing more IT at it; however, as always perhaps we need to take a step back and look more closely at this problem.

Julia Adler-Milstein over at the Harvard Business School has been looking into this issue and she's made some interesting discoveries. She's found that the hope for these EHRs are that they will improve work flow, accuracy, communication with patients, access to medical history, and clinical decision making. As we in IT know, **more than just IT changes** will be needed…

It turns out that studies that have been done by MIT Sloan School's Erik Brynjolfsson and others have shown that organizations (not just health care industries) can only take advantage of new IT capabilities **after they make substantial changes**. Oh, oh – this sounds like work.

The types of changes that organizations need to make include increased training and **increased individual decision making authority**. They also flattened their hierarchies, made better use of their staff, decentralized their teams, and ended up raising the incentives for team performance.

As any CIO knows, IT changes by themselves can't solve business problems. No matter if you are talking about how to solve the U.S. health care crisis or any industries need for more automation, an IT solution will only go so far. Making the rest of the company understand that IT can provide the tools needed to solve a business problem, but that **organizational changes** will also be required, is a fundamental job for the CIO.

Chapter 6

The Problem With Apple: Product Or Platform?

Chapter 6: The Problem With Apple: Product Or Platform?

In the world of IT we deal with lots of different questions: what project to take on, how best to align with the business, how to improve processes. One thing that we don't really spend much time thinking about is if our applications should run on Microsoft or Apple platforms. Hmm, has Apple missed the boat here?

I bring this up as a discussion point because, let's face it, Apple makes some fantastic products. Starting with the Mac, they went on to produce the PowerBook, the Newton (come on, you remember that one), the iPod, the iPhone, etc. However, they've never really been a platform company.

I'm playing games with words here and perhaps I should better explain myself. Michael Cusumano over at the Communications of the ACM gave this some thought awhile back and I think that he was on to something. He defined a platform as being something that had open interfaces and for which further development was encouraged and licensed. Apple doesn't do this.

From an IT perspective, this causes a number of problems. There's no question that Apple products are "sexy" and easy to use. However, since there is all too often only one source for features and applications, an ecosystem comparable to that which developed around Microsoft products never arose.

No big deal you say – Apple products are only found in graphic design shops and educational environments. Well, up until the iPhone came out I would have agreed with you. However, the runaway success of the iPhone and the demand for iPhone apps from the Apple store is starting to make it look like a dominate mobile computing platform.

As more and more of your staff start showing up sporting Apple iPhones, you are going to start to feel pressure to come up with ways to iPhone enable your IT department's apps. This can be done, it's just that you'll find that it's not as easy as connecting a Microsoft PC to your network.

Times are changing and Apple still makes great products. However, since they are not in the business of making platforms you've got your work cut out for you…

Chapter 7

Practical IT Clouds: What To Do AFTER The Hype

Chapter 7: Practical IT Clouds: What To Do AFTER The Hype

Talk about your latest buzz word overkill! Just when the "Web 2.0" madness had just about hit its peak, along came "**Cloud Computing**" and took its crown. It's looking like cloud computing is here to stay, so what's an IT department to do once they get done studying the whole thing?

Your IT department will eventually use cloud computing. There, I've said it. If you don't believe me, then go back and read those words to yourself out-loud several times until you do. **It's coming and there's nothing that you can do to stop it**. Just like outsourcing, it makes good economic sense and so all other objections will be worked out over time.

The idea that organizations can increase their computing power without having to buy, install, maintain, power, and cool more and more boxes is just too attractive to the bean counters to ignore. This puts IT in a tricky spot: our world is getting ready to be **turned upside down** – are you ready?

Here's the problem: a lot of the support jobs that IT does today will go away along with "the boxes". What nobody seems to realize is that they will be replaced by **new IT jobs**. If you're running an IT shop, you'd better be ready!

Here are the new Cloud Computing tasks that are coming your way that you're going to have to find ways to staff:

1. **Extend**: you're going to have to come up with ways to create bridges between your existing network environment and the cloud. Oh, and then you're going to have staff to maintain those bridges.

2. **Pick:** you're going to have to pick a couple of cloud service providers. Once you're in bed with them, you are going to have to have staff to monitor how they are performing and to provide the human interface to fix the issues that always show up.

3. **Monitor**: forget outages, what about day-to-day issues? You are going to need staff to monitor and manage the apps that you have running "in the cloud".

4. **Identify**: who on your staff is allowed to do what? Since the old rules about getting access to boxes no longer apply, you're going to need new rules and new staff to enforce and update them.

5. **Encrypt:** since you are now going to be storing data off site and "out there", encryption becomes more than a nice-to-have, now it's a necessity. Somebody on your staff is going to have to be double checking everything all the time to make sure that it REALLY IS encrypted.

6. **Plan:** for the worst. Data link outages are going to be a much bigger deal then they ever used to be. How will you handle being disconnected from your cloud for an hour, a day, a week? Somebody had better be put in charge of solving this problem and keeping this solution updated.

7. **Mange**: your bandwidth. Now that the link between you and your cloud has become critical to how the business runs, you had better have someone on it at all times.

We're looking at a brave new future. **Do you have the right staff** with the right set of skills in order to make the most of it?

Chapter 8

Unified Communications Is An Opportunity For CIOs To Show Their Value

Chapter 8: Unified Communications Is An Opportunity For CIOs To Show Their Value

The role of a CIO in any organization is to find ways to enable the company **to be more successful**. This can include introducing new products quicker, reacting to changes in the marketplace faster, or even lowering the cost of doing business.

Underlying all of these different ways to assist the business there is one area that every CIO must master first: **providing great internal communications**. An opportunity to radically transform how a firm's employees communicate has arrived and it's time for CIOs to step up and lead the charge.

Just What Is Unified Communications?

"Unified Communications" (UC) is starting to take on all the characteristics of a high-tech buzzword and in the process folks are losing track of just what it really means. If you boil it down to its bare essence, unified communications is all about moving all of your voice, video, and data business communications to **a single network**. Instead of having a phone network, a LAN, and the Internet, you combine all three of these into a single unified (get it?) network that carries all business communication.

Is This Really The Right Time To Be Talking About This?

Hey, there's a recession going on – right? Despite the current economic problems that the world is facing, CIOs still have a job to do and studying and implementing a unified communications solution is a key part of this. The world markets will recover and if the company is left behind while its competition zooms ahead because the company stopped innovating then there's going to be **an opening for a new CIO**.

Nicholas Hoover over at InformationWeek has been asking around and he's found out that:

- 57% of companies have not gotten past the pilot stage
- 86% say that they can make a good business case for it
- 55% admit that their company is confused about the value of UC

What Global Crossing Did

Just in case you need some more motivation to look into what unified communication can do for your firm, how about if we take a look at what the communication company Global Crossing did.

Global Crossing has embraced unified communications in a big way. Their chief operations officer uses it to hold weekly global staff meetings with his 16 direct reports. They use the video conferencing capabilities that they now have. The **savings** of using a unified communications solution for this type of meeting can be calculated in terms of savings on conferencing services, long distance calls, and even travel costs.

Global Crossing has taken unified communications one step further. They've discovered that the real hidden value to this new service is what is called "**presence awareness**" – who's currently there for you to communicate with? They've integrated this functionality into their day-to-day business applications so that people using them will know who they can contact if something goes wrong.

Final Thoughts

All too rarely does an opportunity like this come along that will allow CIOs to clearly demonstrate **their value to the firm**. As existing PBXs and data network components start to become obsolete, there has never been a better time to start to analyze **WHEN** will be the right time to upgrade to a unified communications solution. Your company needs you now...

Chapter 9

First-Mover Advantage: Complex-Event Processing Is What CIOs Need

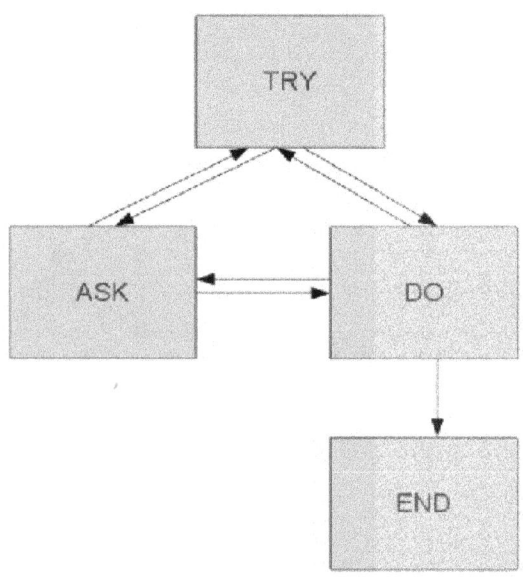

Chapter 9: First-Mover Advantage: Complex-Event Processing Is What CIOs Need

The job of a CIO and the IT department is to equip the rest of the company **to move faster and do more**. One of the ways that a CIO can do this is by staying on top of new and emerging technologies (ex. unified communications).

If such technologies can be implemented in a useful way **BEFORE** the company's competitors can do the same, then the CIO will have done his/her job. Complex-Event Processing looks like it may be another one of those technologies.

What Is "Complex-Event Processing"?

In business, knowledge is power and power is profit. Every business has **multiple streams of information** flowing into it at all times. Information on sales, inventory, returns, web site clicks, weather conditions, bank balances, etc.

For years firms have been processing these information streams individually and in **near-real-time**. These are the core business applications that produce the reports that get sent to senior management each night for them to review the next day. This is better than nothing, but it's not quite enough.

Neal Leavitt writing in the IEEE's Computer magazine points out that today's traditional databases are **not up to the task** of analyzing continuous streams of business data in real-time searching for complex events (events that require more than one data stream to detect).

What is now arriving on the IT scene are general-purpose platforms that provide an IT department with enough processing horsepower to analyze **real-time** business information **simultaneously** across multiple business applications.

What's It Good For?

Complex-event processing gives a firm the ability to spot interconnected business trends and patterns in real-time and then combine this information into complex events that can trigger **alerts** that can be sent to people in the company.

Complex events can include such things as determining when to trade stocks, **detecting fraud as it is happening**, spotting inventory issues before they become a problem, network status monitoring, etc.

Are There Any Risks?

Of course – this is cutting edge technology, there are always risks with this stuff. The current limitations to this type of technology include:

1. **Lack Of Standards:** specifically for the event-pattern detection and rule-based languages for different vendor's products.

2. **Education:** this is new technology and businesses don't fully understand what the products can do nor all of the situations in which they can be applied.

3. **Missing Benchmarks**: No standardized benchmarks currently exist so it's difficult to compare products.

Final Thoughts

Every great business break-through starts with a dream. What could your firm do if you could **analyze all of your business data**

streams in real-time? If the benefit is compelling enough, then perhaps it's time to start looking into how you could apply complex-event processing as a way to get IT to enable the rest of the company to grow quicker, move faster, and do more.

Chapter 10

Web 3.0 Is Coming — Are CIOs Ready?

Chapter 10: Web 3.0 Is Coming – Are CIOs Ready?

Oh Web 2.0, it seems like only yesterday that you arrived – is it possible that already you may be getting ready to be replaced? The answer is not quite yet, but the outline of what the **Web 3.0** is going to look like is starting to firm up. CIOs have been slow to take advantage of all that the Web 2.0 had to offer, will they **lag behind again** when the Web 3.0 shows up?

What Was Web 2.0?

Before we run off and start making predictions about the future of the Internet, maybe it would be a good idea to take just a moment and make sure that we are all on the same page as to just exactly **what the Web 2.0 is / was.**

When the web first showed up (Web 1.0), everyone rushed out and created static web pages. That was a great start, but it got a bit boring because nothing changed without a great deal of effort. Web 2.0 extended what we had by adding blogging, **Wikipedia**, social networking (**MySpace, Facebook, LinkedIn**, etc.) and even microblogging (**Twitter**). This changed everything because all of a sudden things could be easily changed – and they were!

What Is Web 3.0 Going To Be?

So what's next I can hear CIOs and soon-to-be CIOs asking. Dr. Jim Hendler at the Rensselaer Polytechnic Institute has been spending some time thinking about this and he's come up with some interesting ideas. Dr. Hendler points out that it appears to all be based on **Tim Berners-Lee's** (you know, the guy who invented the Web) vision of a semantic web.

In this next iteration of the web, what we're going to see is more and more complex **mashups of data** from different applications being used to deliver data in more useful ways. Dr. Hendler believes that the read-write abilities of Web 2.0 applications will be used to build Web 3.0 applications that operate at the data, not the application level.

What's Going To Make The Web 3.0 Happen?

Before the Web 3.0 can show up, a few critical pieces need to drop into place. Ultimately, what needs to happen is that it has to become easier to integrate web data resources. Here are the **emerging technologies** that are going to allow this to happen:

1. **Resource Description Framework (RDF)**: provides a means to link data from multiple different websites or databases. Uses the SQL-like SPARQL query language.

2. **Uniform Resource Identifiers (URI)**: We already have these – this is how you merge and map data that is found in different locations on the web.

3. **Web Ontology Language (OWL)**: allows relationships to be inferred between data that is stored in different parts of the same application.

Final Thoughts

Rare are the times that CIOs actually have a chance to get in front of a **significant change** before it happens. Right now they have such a chance – Web 3.0 is not here yet, but it's getting ready to arrive.

Spending time now to understand what business problems could be solved or solved better if you had a better description of the data that is available on the web is a necessary first step.

Assigning staff to learn and become experts on the new **Web 3.0 technologies** early on will allow CIOs to have **found a way** to apply IT to enable the rest of the company to grow quicker, move faster, and do more.

Chapter 11

CIO Cloud Computing 101: Who Are The Players?

Chapter 11: CIO Cloud Computing 101: Who Are The Players?

One of the great things about working in the IT field is that whenever things start to get boring, we have the ability to create new **buzzwords** and make things interesting all over again. The arrival of "**Cloud Computing**" on the scene a couple of years ago showed that this cycle has not gone away. Maybe it would be worthwhile to **take a step back** and make sure that we're all on the same page here – what is cloud computing and why should anyone care?

The Many Flavors Of Cloud Computing

Neal Leavitt has spent some time studying cloud computing and has some thoughts for us. A quick definition of just what **cloud computing** is might be a good place for us to start. In olden days (3 years ago), if you wanted to run an application you pretty much had to go out, buy a server, plug it in, load up the software, connect it to a network and then you were in business. **Cloud computing changes all of that.**

Now all you have to do is set up an account with a company who has already done all of the above steps. You can then load your application onto their server(s) using the Internet to reach these servers and **ta-da** you are in business.

There are three main "**flavors**" of cloud computing that users are employing currently:

1. **Thin Clients:** allows you to minimize the processing power / storage needed by the end user's computer and do the "heavy lifting" on servers and storage that are stored elsewhere.

2. **Grid Computing**: allows computers that may be located in completely different locations to be connected together in order to form a single virtual computing system. An example of this would be specialized image processing computers that were linked to a massive image storage system for processing.

3. **Utility Computing**: this is cloud computing in its purest form – CPUs for hire. You pay for what you use and you can use as much as you need. This is a great solution for firms that have seasonal spikes in the amount of data that they have to process.

Who Are The Cloud Computing Service Players?

The list of cloud computing **service providers** is long and seems to be getting longer every day. Here's a partial list with a number of names that you'll probably recognize…

1. Amazon.com's Amazon Web Services (AWS)
2. Google's Google Apps
3. Salesforce.com Force.com
4. Microsoft's Windows Azure
5. AppNexus
6. GoGrid
7. GridLayer
8. Mosso
9. XCalibre Communications

Final Thoughts

Ok, so clearly this is not the final thought on Cloud Computing. I've got a lot more to cover with you, but this is a good place to quit for now. Cloud Computing was treated as a bit of a **novelty** when it first showed up. I mean, who would trust unreliable links to remote computers to run critical corporate apps?

Times have changed and the **economics** of Cloud Computing have also changed to make this a more attractive option. Every CIO needs to be thinking about how his / her IT shop is using computing resources right now and **what role Cloud Computing** could play in the future. Addressing this issue this will mean that CIOs will have **found a way** to apply IT to enable the rest of the company to grow quicker, move faster, and do more.

Chapter 12

CIO Cloud Computing 101: Why Use The Cloud?

Chapter 12: CIO Cloud Computing 101: Why Use The Cloud?

Does anyone besides me remember the big Furby craze that swept the U.S. in the early '90's? People went crazy for these little plush dolls and they started collecting them in hopes that they would one day be valuable. Well, that never happened and a lot of people got stuck with expensive toys that they couldn't get rid of. Is it possible that the current **cloud computing craze** in IT could be another Furby fad that will fade away?

What Kind Of Services Come In A Cloud?

If a CIO can move beyond the hype, he/she needs to spend some time doing their homework in order to find out what kinds of **services** a cloud could offer that their company could make use of. Neal Leavitt has spent some time studying cloud computing and has boiled cloud services down into **four types** of services:

1. **Basic Services**: this is not glamorous, but it may be the most popular type of service that a cloud environment can offer to your business. Basically simple Internet based services such as database functionality and capacity, middleware, and additional storage are used to supplement what your company already has.

2. **IaaS**: Buzz word alert – "Infrastructure As A Service". This is when you are renting a complete computer (CPU, storage, bandwidth, etc.) that you access via the Internet. You would use this infrastructure to run your company's applications on lock-stock-and-barrel.

3. **PaaS**: Platform-as-a-service – provides your firm with a development environment that your IT staff can use to

create new applications for the rest of the company (and your customers) to use. This is computer plus development tools.

4. **SaaS**: Software-as-a-service – this is where you don't care about what the software is running on, you just want to purchase access to the application. The most famous example of this is Salesforce.com's CRM application.

Why Bother With A Cloud?

The Forrester research company has done some investigating and they now claim that most company's data centers are using **less than 50%** of their total capacity. Despite the hype that is currently surrounding cloud computing, Leavitt has uncovered **three very good reasons** for looking into having your firm start to use cloud computing:

1. **Availability**: interestingly enough, despite many firm's misgivings about losing control over their IT equipment, there is a lot to be said to having a professional firm that has the deep pockets needed for redundant systems and tested disaster recovery plans run your IT infrastructure. If you work at a small or even a medium sized firm, this may be especially valuable to you.

2. **Integration Of Applications**: sorry, we can't do anything about those old apps that you are running. However, the new ones that are developed to run in the cloud will almost automatically be easy to integrate because they will use the suite of Web interface languages/tools (SOAP, XML, etc.) that make this easy to do.

3. **Flexibility**: unlike the majority of cell phone vendors in the U.S., currently most cloud computing service providers don't require users to sign long term

contracts that lock them in. This makes it easy to quickly get more cloud resources when your firm needs them.

Final Thoughts

It is all too easy for CIOs who are adverse to change to look at the current excitement over cloud computing and decide that it is **yet another fad** that will fade away in time. The reality is that cloud computing provides several different types of **services** that are useful to any IT department. This can't be ignored.

Additionally, successfully adding cloud computing resources to the company's existing IT infrastructure will mean that a CIO will have **found a way** to apply IT to enable the rest of the company to grow quicker, move faster, and do more.

It's from the forge of failure that the steel of success is formed.

Hard Work Does Not Guarantee Success, But Success Does Not Happen Without Hard Work.

- Dr. Jim Anderson

Create IT Departments That Are Productive And A Valuable Asset To The Rest Of The Company!

Dr. Jim Anderson is available to provide training and coaching on the topics that are the most important to people who have to manage IT departments: how can I build a productive IT department (and keep it together) while at the same time providing the rest of the company with the IT services that they need?

Dr. Anderson believes that in order to both learn and remember what he says, speakers need to laugh. Each one of his speeches is full of fun and humor so that what he says "sticks" with everyone.

Dr. Anderson's CIO SkillsTraining Includes:

1. How to identify and attract the right type of IT workers to your IT department.
2. How to build relationships with the company's senior management in order to get the support that you need?
3. How to stay on top of changing technology and security issues so that you never get surprised?

Dr. Jim Anderson works with over 100 customers per year. To invite Dr. Anderson to work with you, contact him at:

Phone: 813-418-6970 or
Email: jim@BlueElephantConsulting.com

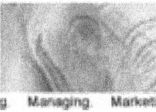

Photo Credits:

Cover - Global Panorama
https://www.flickr.com/photos/121483302@N02/

Chapter 1 - Dan Farber
https://www.flickr.com/photos/farber/

Chapter 2 - Daniel Rehn
https://www.flickr.com/photos/daniel-rehn/

Chapter 3 - Marc Smith
https://www.flickr.com/photos/marc_smith/

Chapter 4 - BBC World Service
https://www.flickr.com/photos/bbcworldservice/

Chapter 5 - Washington State House Republicans
https://www.flickr.com/photos/wahousegop/

Chapter 6 - Zoli Erdos
https://www.flickr.com/photos/zoliblog/

Chapter 7 – theaucitron
https://www.flickr.com/photos/theaucitron/

Chapter 8 - NEC Corporation of America
https://www.flickr.com/photos/neccorp/

Chapter 9 – doryfour
https://www.flickr.com/photos/28738704@N07/

Chapter 10 - Amber Case
https://www.flickr.com/photos/caseorganic/

Chapter 11 - Daniel Spiess
https://www.flickr.com/photos/deegephotos/

Chapter 12 - Jenny Laird
https://www.flickr.com/photos/99095055@N04/

Other Books By The Author

Product Management

- How Product Managers Can Sell More Of Their Product: Tips & Techniques For Product Managers To Better Understand How To Sell Their Product

- How Product Managers Can Sell More Of Their Product: Tips & Techniques For Product Managers To Better Understand How To Sell Their Product

- How To Create A Successful Product That Customers Will Want: Techniques For Product Managers To Boost Product Sales And Increase Customer Satisfaction

- What Product Managers Need To Know About World-Class Product Development: How Product Managers Can Create Successful Products

- How Product Managers Can Learn To Understand Their Customers: Techniques For Product Managers To Better Understand What Their Customers Really Want

- Product Management Secrets: Techniques For Product Managers To Boost Produ Michael Kct Sales And Increase Customer Satisfaction

- Product Development Lessons For Product Managers: How Product Managers Can Create Successful Products

- Customer Lessons For Product Managers: Techniques For Product Managers To Better Understand What Their Customers Really Want

- Product Failure Lessons For Product Managers: Examples Of Products That Have Failed For Product Managers To Learn From

- Communication Skills For Product Managers: The Communication Skills That Product Managers Need To Know How To Use In Order To Have A Successful Product

- How To Have A Successful Product Manager Career: The Things That You Need To Be Doing TODAY In Order To Have A Successful Product Manager Career

- Product Manager Product Success: How to keep your product on track and make it become a success

Public Speaking

- How To Organize A Speech In Order To Make Your Point: How to put together a speech that will capture and hold your audience's attention

- Changing How You Speak To Overcome Your Fear Of Speaking: Change techniques that will transform a speech into a memorable event

- Delivering Excellence: How To Give Presentations That Make A Difference: Presentation techniques that will transform a speech into a memorable event

- Tools Speakers Need In Order To Give The Perfect Speech: What tools to use to create your next speech so that your message will be remembered forever!

- How To Create A Speech That Will Be Remembered

- Secrets To Organizing A Speech For Maximum Impact: How to put together a speech that will capture and hold your audience's attention

- How To Become A Better Speaker By Changing How You Speak: Change techniques that will transform a speech into a memorable event

- How To Give A Great Presentation: Presentation techniques that will transform a speech into a memorable event

- How To Rehearse In Order To Give The Perfect Speech: How to effectively rehearse your next speech to that your message be remembered forever!

- Secrets To Creating The Perfect Speech: How to create a speech that will make your message be remembered forever!

- Secrets To Organizing The Perfect Speech: How to organize the best speech of your life!

- Secrets To Planning The Perfect Speech: How to plan to give the best speech of your life

- How To Show What You Mean During A Presentation: How to use visual techniques to transform a speech into a memorable event

CIO Skills

- Keeping The Barbarians Out: How CIOs Can Secure Their Department and Company: Tips And Techniques For CIOs To Use In Order To Secure Both Their IT

Department And Their Company

- What CIOs Need To Know In Order To Successfully Manage An IT Department: Decision Making Skills That Every CIO Needs To Have In Order To Be Able To Make The Right Choices

- Becoming A Powerful And Effective Leader: Tips And Techniques That IT Managers Can Use In Order To Develop Leadership Skills

- CIO Secrets For Growing Innovation: Tips And Techniques For CIOs To Use In Order To Make Innovation Happen In Their IT Department

- Your Success As A CIO Depends On How Well You Communicate: Tips And Techniques For CIOs To Use In Order To Become Better Communicators

- What CIOs Need To Know About Working With Partners: Techniques For CIOs To Use In Order To Be Able To Successfully Work With Partners

- Critical CIO Management Skills: Decision Making Skills That Every CIO Needs To Have In Order To Be Able To Make The Right Choices

- How CIOs Can Make Innovation Happen: Tips And Techniques For CIOs To Use In Order To Make

Innovation Happen In Their IT Department

- CIO Communication Skills Secrets: Tips And Techniques For CIOs To Use In Order To Become Better Communicators

- Managing Your CIO Career: Steps That CIOs Have To Take In Order To Have A Long And Successful Career

- CIO Business Skills: How CIOs can work effectively with the rest of the company!

IT Manager Skills

- How To Build High Performance IT Teams: Tips And Techniques That IT Managers Can Use In Order To Develop Productive Teams

- Save Yourself, Save Your Job – How To Manage Your IT Career: Secrets That IT Managers Can Use In Order To Have A Successful Career

- Growing Your CIO Career: How CIOs Can Work With The Entire Company In Order To Be Successful

- How IT Managers Can Make Innovation Happen: Tips And Techniques For IT Managers To Use In

Order To Make Innovation Happen In Their Teams

- Staffing Skills IT Managers Must Have: Tips And Techniques That IT Managers Can Use In Order To Correctly Staff Their Teams

- Secrets Of Effective Leadership For IT Managers: Tips And Techniques That IT Managers Can Use In Order To Develop Leadership Skills

- IT Manager Career Secrets: Tips And Techniques That IT Managers Can Use In Order To Have A Successful Career

- IT Manager Budgeting Skills: How IT Managers Can Request, Manage, Use, And Track Their Funding

- Secrets Of Managing Budgets: What IT Managers Need To Know In Order To Understand How Their Company Uses Money

Negotiating

- Exploring How To Get The Deal That You Want In A Negotiation: How To Develop The Skill Of Exploring What Is Possible In A Negotiation In Order To Reach The Best Possible Deal

- Use The Power Of Arguing To Win Your Next Negotiation: How To Develop The Skill Of Effective Arguing In A Negotiation In Order To Get The Best Possible Outcome

- Learn How To Signal In Your Next Negotiation: How To Develop The Skill Of Effective Signaling In A Negotiation In Order To Get The Best Possible Outcome

- Learn The Skill Of Exploring In A Negotiation: How To Develop The Skill Of Exploring What Is Possible In A Negotiation In Order To Reach The Best Possible Deal

- Learn How To Argue In Your Next Negotiation: How To Develop The Skill Of Effective Arguing In A Negotiation In Order To Get The Best Possible Outcome|

- How To Open Your Next Negotiation: How To Start A Negotiation In Order To Get The Best Possible Outcome

- Preparing For Your Next Negotiation: What You Need To Do BEFORE A Negotiation Starts In Order To Get The Best Possible Deal

- Learn How To Package Trades In Your Next Negotiation

- All Good Things Come To An End: How To Close A Negotiation - How To Develop The Skill Of Closing In Order To Get The Best Possible Outcome From A Negotiation

- Take No Prisoners In Your Next Negotiation: How To Start A Negotiation In Order To Get The Best Possible Outcome

Miscellaneous

- How To Heal A Broken Leg – Fast!: Understanding how to deal with a broken leg in order to start walking again quickly

- How Software Defined Networking (SDN) Is Going To Change Your World Forever: The Revolution In Network Design And How It Affects You

- The Power Of Virtualization: How It Affects Memory, Servers, and Storage: The Revolution In Creating Virtual Devices And How It Affects You

- The Internet-Enabled Successful School District Superintendent: How To Use The Internet To Boost

Parental Involvement In Your Schools

- Power Distribution Unit (PDU) Secrets: What Everyone Who Works In A Data Center Needs To Know!

- Making The Jump: How To Land Your Dream Job When You Get Out Of College!

- How To Use The Internet To Create Successful Students And Involved Parents

How CIOs Can Stay On Top Of The Changes In The Technology That Powers The Company

> This book has been written with one goal in mind – to show you how you can stay on top of all of the changes that are occurring in the technologies that your company uses. Master these technologies today and your company will thank you!
>
> **Let's Make Your CIO Career A Success!**

What You'll Find Inside:

- **CRM NEWS: THE BUSINESS OF INFORMATION TECHNOLOGY IS CHANGING**

- **PRACTICAL IT CLOUDS: WHAT TO DO AFTER THE HYPE**

- **UNIFIED COMMUNICATIONS IS AN OPPORTUNITY FOR CIOS TO SHOW THEIR VALUE**

- **WEB 3.0 IS COMING – ARE CIOS READY?**

Dr. Jim Anderson brings his 25 years of real-world experience to this book. He's been a senior IT executive at some of the world's largest firms. He's going to show you what you need to do (and not do!) in order to make your CIO career a success!

www.ingramcontent.com/pod-product-compliance
Lightning Source LLC
Chambersburg PA
CBHW061206180526
45170CB00002B/978